ZION BENTON PUBLIC
LIBRARY DISTRICT
Zion, Illinois 60099

DEMCO

A LERNER BIOGRAPHY

ella Fitzgerald

first lady of song

katherine krohn

Lerner Publications Company/Minneapolis

For Hannah

Lerner Publications Company
A division of Lerner Publishing Group
241 First Avenue North
Minneapolis, MN 55401 U.S.A.

Website address: www.lernerbooks.com

Library of Congress Cataloging-in-Publication Data

Krohn, Katherine E.
    Ella Fitzgerald : first lady of song / by Katherine Krohn.
        p.   cm.—(Lerner biographies)
    Includes bibliographical references, discography, and index.
        Summary: A biography of the celebrated jazz singer, known especially for her scat singing and "songbook" recordings of the works of many major American composers.
        ISBN 0-8225-4933-6 (lib. bdg. : alk. paper)
        1. Fitzgerald, Ella—Juvenile literature. 2. Singers—United States—Biography—Juvenile literature. [1. Fitzgerald, Ella. 2. Singers. 3. Jazz. 4. Afro-Americans—Biography. 5. Women—Biography.] I. Title.
ML3930.F5 K76 2001
782.42165'092—dc21   00-009166

Manufactured in the United States of America
1 2 3 4 5 6 – JR – 06 05 04 03 02 01

Contents

Early in her career, Ella Fitzgerald won over crowds with her clear, sweet voice.

𝒢 ONE 𝒢

AMATEUR HOUR

Just don't give up trying to do what you really want to do. Where there's love and inspiration, I don't think you can go wrong.

–Ella Fitzgerald

Put your hands together for Ella Fitzgerald!"

Seventeen-year-old Ella Fitzgerald had never felt more scared, or more excited, in her life. She had never been onstage before. She had never sung in front of an audience, and she knew that the folks who came to Amateur Night at the Apollo Theater in New York's Harlem neighborhood weren't an easy crowd to please. Her knees shaking, her hands jumpy with nervous energy, Ella followed the emcee's cue. She hurried to the microphone, knowing her voice would be broadcast live over Radio WMCA.

On that evening of November 21, 1934, the noisy crowd quieted down to stare at the odd-looking character onstage. She was a tall, large-framed girl with long, skinny legs. Her black hair was a tangled mess. She wore men's boots with a faded dress that looked like it hadn't been washed in weeks.

"Hey, honey, where'd you get them clothes?" someone shouted.

Ella thought about bolting, but she didn't. She gathered her courage and began to sing her first number, "The Object of My Affection."

Ella began singing the song, her voice pure and beautiful. But then her voice cracked. She stopped singing abruptly. Her accompaniment, the Benny Carter Orchestra, stopped playing. The crowd began to rumble. She heard people whispering. Someone laughed.

Ella took a deep breath and started again. This time, she sang the song all the way through. The people in the audience listened attentively. They had never heard of Ella Fitzgerald before, but this girl could really *sing*. Her clear voice, though untrained, was excellent. And, even though she was young, insecure, and unkempt, Ella had what stars have—magnetism. When she finished, the crowd clapped loudly and flashed reassuring smiles. Encouraged, Ella sang another popular song of the day, "Judy."

After her act, Ella went backstage and watched the remaining contestants, singers and dancers, perform. She hoped she would win the twenty-five-dollar first prize. She desperately needed the money.

Ella's mother had died two years earlier. Her father had abandoned the family when Ella was a small child, and her stepfather was also deceased. Ella was on her own, and she needed to make her own way somehow.

At the end of the Apollo amateur contests, the emcee would point at each contestant, and whoever received the loudest applause from the audience won the contest. The winner would receive twenty-five dollars and an even greater prize—the opportunity to perform in the next week's show.

The night of Ella's stage debut, the emcee pointed to the contestants one by one. As each performer took a bow, the audience clapped moderately. But when he came to Ella, the crowd roared. Without question, young Ella Fitzgerald won the contest and the twenty-five dollars, a fortune to her at the time.

Breaking the usual agreement, however, the club managers didn't invite Ella to come back the next week to appear in the show. Although she was talented, Ella just didn't fit the image of a nightclub performer. She didn't have enough money to have her hair styled or to buy a fancy dress. All she had to wear were her worn street clothes. The Apollo was a

Ella relied on the strength of her voice for her early performances. Later, her glamorous look (left) *helped her win over even more audiences.*

posh, trendy club, popular with celebrities of the time, such as Joan Crawford and Bob Hope. Image mattered. Money mattered. And looks mattered most of all.

Ella didn't ask the Apollo managers why they hadn't asked her to return. She was just thrilled to have been paid for singing. And she wasn't a girl who would give up easily. She knew she'd be back onstage again, though she wasn't sure where or when.

"Someday you're going to see me in the headlines," Ella told her friends. "I'm going to be famous."

President Ronald Reagan presented Ella with a National Medal of Arts award at the White House in 1985.

"Oh yeah, sure," her friends laughed.

Ella knew something her friends didn't know: she was destined to become one of the most celebrated jazz singers of all time. In her lifetime, Ella Fitzgerald recorded more than two hundred top-selling albums. She won more Grammy awards than any other female vocalist in history, and she received the National Medal of Arts from the president of the United States. Her climb to the top wouldn't be easy, but somehow Ella knew she would get there.

The Original Dixieland Jazz Band recorded the first jazz tunes in New York City in 1917, the year Ella was born.

✂ TWO ✎

ELLA JANE

In 1917 the United States entered World War I, siding with France, Great Britain, Russia, Japan, and Italy to fight Germany, Austria-Hungary, and Turkey. Woodrow Wilson was serving his second term as U.S. president. In the same year, astronomers were discussing the new theory of black holes, American women were just two years away from winning the right to vote, and the Original Dixieland Jazz Band made the first jazz recordings in New York City.

On Wednesday, April 25, 1917, Ella Jane Fitzgerald was born in Newport News, Virginia, a bustling Atlantic Ocean shipping port. Ella's parents, William Fitzgerald, thirty-two, and Temperance "Tempie" Williams, twenty-three, were both native Virginians. William drove a transfer wagon, a vehicle that moved railroad freight. Tempie worked in a laundry.

William, Tempie, and baby Ella lived in a rented house at

2050 Madison Avenue in Newport News. Times were hard for the family. William and Tempie struggled to get by. When Ella was just a toddler, William abandoned Tempie and Ella.

Within a year, Tempie found a new partner. Joseph Da Silva, a tall, heavyset man, was a first-generation immigrant from Portugal. Joseph, like Tempie, was ambitious, hard-working, and tired of being poor. In 1921 Joseph and Tempie gathered up their few possessions and moved with the young Ella to Yonkers, New York, near New York City.

In the 1920s, many African Americans from the South migrated to northern cities in search of opportunity. Like others who relocated to the urban centers, Joseph and Tempie hoped to find good jobs and a better life. Unfortunately, many of those who joined "the great migration" met with disappointment and continuing poverty.

The family didn't have enough money to rent a house or an apartment. Instead, they rented a room in a big brick building at 27 Clinton Street in Yonkers. Before long, Joseph landed a job at a nearby sugar factory. Tempie also found work in the neighborhood, at the Silver Lining Laundry. The couple worked hard, saved whatever money they could, and waited for better times.

In 1923 Tempie gave birth to her second child, Frances. Even though Ella was six years older than the baby, she was happy to have a sister.

In September of that year, Ella started school at Public School 10, just a few blocks from her house. Most of the children Ella met at P.S. 10 came from poor families, like hers.

Two years later, Ella's family moved into an apartment a few blocks away. In this neighborhood, African American, Italian, Irish, Eastern European, and Greek families lived side by side.

"We were all in the same boat, whites and blacks," remembered one of Ella's childhood friends. "We were poorer than the poor today. But we all got on, that's the difference. Today it's a different story."

Ella's best friend was Rose Sarubbi, an Italian girl who lived two blocks away. After school, Ella often went over to Rose's house. Sometimes she stayed for dinner. Ella grew to love the lasagna, spaghetti, chicken cacciatore, and other Italian dishes that Rose's mother prepared.

Tempie continued to work full time at the laundry. After work, she came home and cooked, cleaned the apartment, and cared for her family. Annette Miller, who lived in the same apartment building as Ella, remembered Ella's mother: "All the kids used to play together, and her mother would come home from work and . . . stop and talk with us all. She was a very nice lady, a very fine lady who used to work very hard."

Tempie and Joseph were a religious couple. The family attended the Bethany African Methodist Episcopal Church in Yonkers. Ella went to Bible class and Sunday school. Ella first learned that she could sing in church, singing hymns. She eventually joined the church choir.

Like many popular singers, including Aretha Franklin and Whitney Houston, Ella got her start singing in church. She liked to sing spirituals and gospel, high-energy, soulful, rhythmic music. "Gospel singing is jazz gussied up and dressed in the clothes of a lamb," music critic Whitney Balliett once said. "Gospel singers use jazz rhythms and inflections, and they often use them outrageously."

Ella would sing out loud and clear, releasing all the feeling in her heart. In the choir, Ella received her first vocal training, and she began singing in front of a live audience—the congregation at Bethany Church—each and every Sunday.

The Cotton Club in New York City was one of the premier jazz venues during the Jazz Age of the 1920s.

When Ella Fitzgerald was growing up, television didn't exist. Families gathered around their radios in the evening and listened to favorite radio shows of the time, such as the Western drama *The Lone Ranger.* In 1927, when jazz musician and composer Duke Ellington and his orchestra began broadcasting live from the Cotton Club in Harlem, a whole new musical world opened up for Ella.

She loved this hot new musical trend. Jazz was different from any other type of music. Jazz was inventive, and it was improvisational. Players made up new tunes and variations on songs and no one could predict how a particular piece of music would turn out.

Jazz emerged in the late 1800s among African American musicians who drew on a variety of musical sources, including minstrel and vaudeville traditions and ragtime piano music. The earliest jazz bands formed in New Orleans, Louisiana, using instruments such as trumpets, trombones, saxophones, drums, and piano. The players jammed (played on the spur of the moment) in an improvised style—the hallmark of jazz. Their music was copied by the Original Dixieland Jazz Band, a white group that was the first to record jazz.

Several styles of jazz evolved over the years. Ella especially enjoyed swing, the orchestrated big band music that

As the new style of jazz music, called swing, became popular in the 1930s, swing dancing became the rage in clubs such as the Savoy Ballroom in Harlem.

Connee Boswell (center) *was one of Ella's early musical influences. Connee and her sisters, Vet* (left) *and Martha* (right), *performed as the Boswell Sisters.*

was fun to dance to. Big bands played harmonized arrangements for larger ensembles, such as three or four saxophones, three or four brass instruments, and one or more drums. Benny Goodman, Woody Herman, Tommy and Jimmy Dorsey, and Glenn Miller were leaders of popular big bands in the 1930s.

Besides jazz performers, Ella liked the popular singers Bing Crosby and Arthur Tracy, who called himself "the Street Singer" and had a radio show on CBS. But Ella's favorite pop vocalist was Connee Boswell, one of the singers in a sister act called the Boswell Sisters. The three Boswell Sisters, all classically trained musicians, sang in close harmony. They paved the way for future trios, quartets, and quintets. The

Trombonist Glenn Miller (foreground) *led a popular big band in the 1930s. Big bands, or orchestras, as they were sometimes called, used large ensembles of musicians.*

Andrews Sisters, popular in the 1940s, modeled themselves after the Boswells. Ella listened to Connee's songs so many times that she knew them all by heart. She sang them over and over again, trying to make her voice sound just like Connee's.

As much as Ella liked to sing, she loved to dance even more. As a young teen, she dreamed of becoming a famous dancer. Sometimes she and her friend Charles Gulliver would ride the subway into New York City and sneak into one of the grown-up dance halls, like Harlem's Savoy Ballroom, to learn the latest dance steps. Ella tried to move like Snake Hips Tucker, a famous Harlem dancer who wiggled his hips like a snake.

Back in their neighborhood, they would teach other kids the dances they had learned, such as the Susie Q. and the Shuffle Off to Buffalo. Ella and Charles usually practiced their dance steps on the streets and sidewalks. They made up their own routines. Passersby often stopped and watched them, impressed.

Josephine Attanasio, one of Ella's classmates at Benjamin Franklin Junior High School, remembered Ella singing for the kids at school. "It would be at lunchtime or in the morning when we were outside the building. She would be standing up against the wall, and she would be popping and shaking and swaying, dancing to herself. . . . " Josephine said. "[Ella] would just be out there, and we'd just hang around watching her. She just smiled all the time, just shaking her shoulders and singing. She had dangling earrings, those big hoops, and broken-down shoes. We were poor in those days."

When they were fifteen, Ella and Charles found work doing what they loved. Small clubs in Yonkers hired them to dance on Saturday nights. "They might have somebody who could sing, somebody who could dance, somebody who played an instrument or a comedian," Charles remembered. "We danced, and that's what we did to earn a few pennies."

Ella in the 1930s

❧ THREE ❧

Wayward Winds

In early 1932, when Ella was fifteen, her hardworking mother died suddenly of a heart attack. Tempie was only thirty-eight years old.

Ella was devastated. She had been very close to her mother. Like many young people who are faced with unbearable grief, Ella tried to focus on other things. She plunged into her dancing. She practiced her routines many hours a day with her friend Charles. She held tight to her dream of becoming a famous dancer.

Ella's stepfather, Joe, already a strict parent, became even more controlling after Tempie's death. Some people believe that Joe was abusive toward Ella. Charles Gulliver later commented, "He wasn't taking good care of her."

Later in the year, Tempie's sister Virginia Henry removed Ella from her stepfather's home and brought her to live with her and her daughter, Georgiana, on West 145th Street in Harlem. Aunt Virginia became Ella's foster mother.

Ella grew close to her cousin Georgiana. She also stayed in touch with her sister, Frances, who still lived with Joe in Yonkers. Ella visited Frances as often as she could. When Ella's stepfather died of a heart attack later that year, Frances joined Ella at Aunt Virginia's home.

Ella had been an excellent and well-behaved student. After her mother's death, however, she was full of sadness, and she expressed her grief as anger and rage. She sometimes acted sassy and disrespectful.

After her mother died, Ella lived with her Aunt Virginia in Harlem. Outdoor markets were common in the neighborhood.

Ella began to skip school. By mid-1934, at age seventeen, she had dropped out of school entirely. She began running numbers (gambling) in the illegal lottery sponsored by the Mafia, a secret criminal organization. She also became a look-out for a house of prostitution, warning the women inside if the police were around.

Ella's risky, law-breaking behavior came to an end when she was picked up by the police. But the criminal justice system didn't place her in a better situation. There is some question about where the family court sent Ella. Some biographers believe that Ella was enrolled in the Riverdale Children's Association, formerly called the Colored Orphan Asylum, in Riverdale-on-Hudson, New York.

Other researchers believe that she was not sent to the Riverdale orphanage but to the New York Training School for Girls in Hudson, New York, a reform school for female minors. The training school housed girls who were "wayward" or "in need of supervision." Most of the girls had done nothing more serious than skip school or run away from home. Others were simply poor kids whose parents didn't have enough money to take care of them.

Biographers agree that in the fall of 1934, Ella ran away from the institution and vowed never to return. She wanted to go back to her aunt's house, but she feared that the police would find her. Instead, Ella returned to the life she knew on the streets of Harlem. There she had freedom, if nothing else.

Cab Calloway (foreground) was a popular Harlem jazz musician in the 1930s.

❧ FOUR ❧

LEAD ME TO HARLEM

New York's Harlem neighborhood sits in upper Manhattan between 96th and 155th Streets. Park Avenue marks the area's eastern edge, and Amsterdam Avenue is its western boundary. Much of Harlem was constructed during a building boom in the early 1900s. At about the same time, New York began to replace Chicago as the center for jazz music—and Harlem was the home of jazz.

From its beginnings, jazz was tied to the new technologies of record production and radio, which brought the new music to a wide audience. Radio also introduced white audiences to many black performers at a time when African Americans were still treated as second-class citizens in the United States. Laws required black people to sit at the back of the bus, and many restaurants, hotels, and theaters refused to serve black customers. Historian Ann Douglas noted, "From the very beginning, jazz is recorded. It is broadcast on radio. . . . What radios and records mean for black musicians is that they can now go into homes where they could never appear as social guests."

By the 1930s, record production agencies and radio stations had popped up all over New York City, and jazz clubs flourished in Harlem. White audiences poured into the clubs to hear popular jazz musicians like the flamboyant singer Cab Calloway and the trumpeter and vocalist Louis Armstrong. According to Ann Douglas, serious European composers and musicians embraced jazz music, seeing it as the American classical music. "Europe was saying, 'Get out of my way. Lead me to Harlem. Lead me to black music'—because that's where the action was."

The 1920s jazz craze accompanied a blossoming social, artistic, and political movement called the Harlem Renaissance, which celebrated African American culture. Black writers including James Weldon Johnson, Countee Cullen, Claude McKay, Zora Neale Hurston, and Langston Hughes created the first body of literature in the United States that described black people's experience from a black perspective.

W. E. B. DuBois, editor of a magazine called *The Crisis,* was an outspoken political leader during the Harlem Renaissance. DuBois encouraged blacks to reject white culture and to embrace their African heritage and cultural pride. But DuBois did not like jazz, which he considered crude and unrefined. He preferred spirituals, the soulful music originally sung by black slaves.

DuBois wasn't alone in his dislike of jazz. Other African Americans, especially those in the upper class, rejected the music. But writer Langston Hughes argued that critics of jazz needed only to listen to the deep feeling in Bessie Smith's blues singing, for instance, to get a sense of real black culture and life.

Some critics, black and white, called jazz the "devil's music" because they believed it caused young people to dance, drink, and act wild. Despite such opposition, jazz music flourished. By the 1930s, jazz had a wider audience than ever before, and it started to lose its association with youthful "wild" behavior.

During the Great Depression of the 1930s, many of the artists who had created the Harlem Renaissance left New York or had to struggle to earn a living. The Great Depression, a national economic crisis, affected most citizens in the United States, especially those who were poor or middle class.

W. E. B. DuBois used his writing to express his hopes for improved conditions for African Americans.

HARLEM SLANG

By the time jazz came into full bloom in the United States in the 1920s and 1930s, African Americans in New York's Harlem neighborhood shared a dialect known informally as Harlem slang. Most of the jazz musicians and followers within Ella's "hep" jazz circle—including Ella herself—probably used Harlem slang.

Following is a sampling of popular slang expressions from the Jazz Age. Some of these expressions are still used.

Apple—Harlem

Barbecue—girlfriend; a beauty

Beat it out—play it hot, emphasize the rhythm

Beat up the chops (or the gums)—to be talkative

Beef—to say, to state ("He beefed to me that....")

Bible—the gospel truth

Blew their wigs—to be very excited or enthusiastic

Blip—something very good

Break it up—to thrill an audience

Bust your conk—to work hard, to give it all you've got

Canary or Chirp—a female vocalist

Cat—musician

Cogs—sunglasses

Crumb crushers—teeth

Cut out—to leave

Dime note—ten-dollar bill

Final—to go home ("I finaled to my pad.")

Frisking the whiskers—warming up for a swing session

Frolic pad—theater or nightclub

Front, Drape, Threads, or Vine—a suit of clothes or a costume

Fry—to get hair straightened

Gammin'—showing off or acting like a flirt

Gasser—outstanding ("When it comes to singing, that wren is a gasser.")

Gimme some skin—to shake hands

Got your boots on—to be wise, to be a "hep cat"

Gravy—profits

Grease—to eat

Ground grippers—shoes

Hard—fine, good ("That's a hard zoot suit you're wearing.")

Hep cat—a cool guy who understands jive or slang

Hide beater or Skin beater—a drummer

Hummer—exceptionally good ("Man, that canary is a hummer.")

Igg—to ignore ("Don't igg me, pops!")

In the groove—perfect

Jack, Pops, or Gate—male friends
Jam—improvised swing music; to play swing music
Jeff or Icky—a pest or a bore
Jelly—anything free, on the house
Jive—Harlem speech or slang ("Are you hep to the jive, Jack?")
Joint is jumping—the place is lively, the club is leaping with fun
Jumped in port—arrived in town
Kick—pocket ("I've got a dime note in my kick.")
Killer-diller—a great thrill
Land o' darkness—Harlem
Licks—musical phrases
Main kick—the stage
Main on the hitch—husband
Man in gray—mail carrier
Mash me a fin—give me five dollars
Mellow—excellent, cool
Melted out—to have no money
Off the cob—corny, out of date
Ride—to swing, to keep perfect tempo in playing or singing
Riff—a hot lick or musical phrase
Rug cutter—a great dancer
Send—to make happy ("That riff sends me, Gate!")
Set of seven brights—one week
Sky piece—hat
Slide your jib—to talk freely
Spoutin'—talking too much
Take off—to play a solo
The man—the police
Togged to the bricks—dressed up
Too much—the best, the greatest
Trilly—to leave ("Well, I guess I'll trilly.")
Truck—to go somewhere ("I think I'll truck on down to the Cotton Club.")
Twister to the slammer—put the key in the door; open the door
Two cents—two dollars
Unhep or Square—not cool
Whipped up—worn out, exhausted
Wren or Queen—a woman
Yard dog—badly attired, unattractive male or female
Zoot—exaggerated
Zoot suit—an oversized suit

Many people lost their businesses or jobs during the depression, which began with the stock market crash in 1929 and lasted well into the 1930s. In 1933 one in every four American workers was unemployed.

The depression brought other changes to Harlem as well. Landlords who had once refused to rent to black tenants changed their minds as it became more difficult to fill their apartments. To save money, two or three families often shared one apartment.

By the end of the 1930s, Harlem was the largest exclusively African American community in the United States. The ritzy Harlem theaters and dance halls, once whites-only establishments, were finally admitting black patrons. Black people bought some of the clubs and catered to a black clientele. The Harlem establishments that featured jazz musicians grew and prospered.

Ever since she was a little girl, Ella Fitzgerald had wanted to be part of the Harlem music and dance scene. Living on the streets of Harlem, she was probably more a part of the scene than she cared to be. Ella bought food with whatever change she made from dancing on the street or in clubs. She was skinny from not eating regularly, and she was dirty because she had nowhere to bathe. She scrambled to find a place to sleep and often relied on the kindness of people she met on the street.

"She lived with people she talked to, and she ate with them, and she slept wherever she could—that's how she made a living," said one of Ella's friends.

On bad days, Ella just felt tired and discouraged. On good days, she turned her frustrations into energy. She was young, hopeful, and very talented. She wasn't going to give up.

Ella entered the Amateur Night contest at the Apollo

Theater as the result of a bet with two of her girlfriends. The three girls had decided to draw straws to see who would go onstage. Ella had drawn the short straw. At first she thought she would enter the contest as a dancer. At the last minute, she decided to enter as a singer because, unlike the other dancers, she didn't have a special costume.

Ella was surprised to win the twenty-five-dollar prize in the contest. From then on, she began to think of herself as a singer instead of a dancer. The ability to sing well had always come easily to her. She didn't realize, at least right away, that singing didn't come so easily to everyone.

Ella tried her luck again in an amateur contest at the

Ella gave one of her early amateur performances at the Lafayette Theatre in Harlem.

Lafayette Theatre in December 1934. The audiences at the Lafayette were known for their merciless attitude toward amateur performers. If they didn't like an act, they made it known.

Ella decided to try out a new song for her performance at the Lafayette. As she walked onto the stage, she told the piano player that she intended to sing "Lost in a Fog." The pianist had never heard of the song.

"You just start, honey, I'll follow you," he said.

Ella eyed the crowd nervously. She had a bad feeling about this night. She started to sing, but about halfway through the refrain, she forgot the words. She stumbled with the lyrics and stopped singing. The piano player stopped playing.

The result was disastrous. "They booed me off the stage," recalled Ella.

Although Ella left the Lafayette in tears that night, she persevered. In January 1935, she entered another amateur contest, at a theater called the Harlem Opera House. This time, Ella decided not to risk singing a new song. She stuck with one of her dependable favorites, "Judy." Ella sang with more confidence than ever, and the crowd loved her. She won first prize and a week's engagement at the theater.

A local newspaper, the *New York Age,* announced the upcoming acts at the Harlem Opera House, mentioning "Ella Fitzgerald, . . . a prize winner at a recent audition contest at the Harlem Opera House." Ella was thrilled. She had never seen her name in print before. A few days later, she spotted a poster for the Harlem Opera House. The name "Ella Fitzgerald" was in small print at the bottom. She would be performing with the Tiny Bradshaw Band and others.

She prepared for the big night by getting her hair styled. "[At the time] Ella's hair was . . . left natural," remembered

Warryn Nottage, whose mother was a childhood friend of Ella's. "She came to my grandma, who proceeded to curl her hair with little 'chorus girl' curls, which she wore for performances for years after."

On the night of her first performance at the Harlem Opera House, on Friday, February 15, Ella was practically on fire with excitement. The theater was full of fun-loving, rowdy customers who were ready to hear good jazz. Ella was the last act of the evening. She intended to give the audience something to remember. Although she was nervous, she couldn't wait to sing.

"They put me on right at the end, when everybody had their coats and was getting ready to leave," Ella said. "Tiny said, 'Ladies and gentlemen, here is the young girl that's been winning all the contests,' and they came back and took their coats off and sat down again."

Wearing a simple gingham dress, frozen to her spot at the microphone, Ella sang three Connee Boswell tunes. The crowd at the Harlem Opera House cheered and clapped. It didn't matter to them that she didn't have a beautiful gown or that her hair wasn't fixed in the latest style. They liked her singing—her clear, pure voice.

Soon after Ella's gig, or engagement, at the Harlem Opera House, a famous New York bandleader named Chick Webb announced that he was interested in hiring a female singer to accompany his jazz orchestra. Chick Webb was a small-framed, humpbacked drummer from Baltimore, Maryland. He had tuberculosis of the spine, a painful disease that would only worsen in time. At age twenty-six, Chick also had a reputation—as the best jazz drummer in New York City, and maybe the world. He led Chick Webb and His Orchestra, a popular big band.

Many critics thought Chick Webb (center) *was the best drummer in New York City. His band, Chick Webb and His Orchestra, often played at the elegant Savoy Ballroom in the 1930s.*

Webb's booking managers, Moe Gale and Charlie Buchanan, felt that a "girl singer" would attract business. Gale and Buchanan encouraged Webb to find a vocalist in time for the band's next performance at the fashionable Savoy Ballroom in Harlem.

Webb asked Charles Linton, a charismatic, handsome ballad singer who sang with Webb's band, to find a female singer who could do swing music. Webb also requested that she be attractive.

Linton started his search for a vocalist to audition for Chick Webb and His Orchestra. He asked a friend, an Italian woman he knew from the chorus at the Harlem Opera House, "Do you know of a beautiful girl who does swing tunes?"

The woman thought for a minute. "No, I don't," she said. "But there's that little girl who won first prize at the Apollo, and her name's Ella."

Linton perked up. The woman explained that Ella didn't have a phone number or an address—she lived on the street.

He hesitated. A homeless girl? What would Chick say?

"Bring her to me," Linton said.

Ella's career took off when she began singing with Chick Webb's band.

❧ FIVE ❧

SWING SISTER

They tell me you won first prize at the Apollo Theater," Charles Linton said to eighteen-year-old Ella Fitzgerald.

"Yeees," Ella said shyly. She felt self-conscious and scared. She wondered why she had been asked to meet Charles Linton at the Harlem Opera House.

"Sing me the song you won first prize with," said Linton.

Ella felt like she had a frog in her throat, she was so nervous. She sang "Judy" for Linton. When she finished, she was sure she had done a lousy job.

"Well," he said, "your voice is soft, but that's all right. The mike will bring it out. Do you have an encore?"

"Yeees," said Ella. She started to sing "The Object of My Affection," but Linton cut her off in midverse. "That's all right," he said. He was impressed. "Come on up and I'll introduce you to Chick."

Linton knocked on Webb's dressing room door. He poked his head in and said, "Chick, I want you to listen to her sing." He gestured toward Ella.

Ella cowered in the doorway. She saw him staring at her dirty clothes. She knew she probably smelled bad—she hadn't had a bath in a long time.

Webb took Linton inside his dressing room, out of earshot from Ella. He grabbed Linton's collar and whispered angrily, "You're not puttin' that on my bandstand! No, no, no. Out!"

Meanwhile, Ella waited silently. She didn't know what Webb was saying to Linton, but she figured it wasn't good.

Charlie Buchanan, Webb's manager, knocked on the door of the dressing room. Buchanan was in charge of hiring musicians and vocalists to play with Chick Webb's band, and he had been the one who suggested that Webb hire a female singer.

Buchanan shot a glance at Ella. "No, no. Out!" he said.

Luckily for Ella, Charles Linton was on her side. "If you don't listen to her, I will quit!" he shouted.

Later he wondered why he had done that—he didn't want to lose his job, and he didn't even know Ella. But he had a feeling about her. He thought she had great potential, and he felt sorry for her. "She wasn't in any condition to accept any job anyplace," he said. "She was scuffling and didn't have any place to go."

"Oh, no," said Buchanan, astounded at Linton's words. He didn't want to lose one of his most popular singers. "Okay, okay," he reluctantly agreed.

Webb still didn't want Ella, but he knew Buchanan was the boss. Buchanan made a deal with Linton: Ella could sing with the Chick Webb band when they played at the Savoy Ballroom in two weeks. In the meantime, Ella could learn the ropes. "If the public likes her, we'll keep her. And if not, *out! No Pay!*" Buchanan said.

The next week was busy for Ella, but even busier for Charles Linton. Somehow, over the next few days, he had to turn Ella into a stylish nightclub performer—Savoy material.

First, he thought, Ella needed a place to live. The female vocalist for Chick Webb and His Orchestra couldn't be sleeping on the sidewalk. Charles found Ella a room in his apartment house, at 122nd Street and Seventh Avenue in Harlem. He also made arrangements for Ella to run a tab at the nearby Hollywood Restaurant. He would pay her bill at the end of each month so she could eat regular meals. After renting the room and fronting some money to the restaurant, Charles didn't have enough money left to buy Ella something decent to wear onstage. He assured her that she could buy some new clothes after she got paid at the Savoy.

The Chick Webb orchestra was playing for a week at the Harlem Opera House. Each night during the gig, Ella sat attentively and listened to the show. She memorized every song. She paid close attention to Linton's singing style and the way he bantered with the audience between songs. She watched the way he moved, the place he stood, the gestures he made with his arms. Ella intended to perform perfectly during her "trial run" at the Savoy.

"Hey, Sis, where'd you get those clothes?" one of the musicians in the band asked Ella.

"Sis, what's with that hairdo?" asked another.

Ella laughed. The band members had immediately taken a liking to her, and she to them. They called her Sis, and they liked to tease her—especially about her appearance. But behind their comments was serious concern. Although Ella had been hanging around the band for a few days and her first major gig was coming up soon, she still looked a little disheveled and dirty. The musicians knew that she didn't stand a chance in show business if she didn't "clean up her act."

Trombonist Sandy Williams, a serious, sometimes grumpy man, took Ella under his wing. He knew that she had lost her parents, and, like Linton, he wanted to help her. Williams showed Ella how to make herself presentable. He bought her some soap and told her to use it.

By the time Ella stepped onto the stage at the Savoy Ballroom with Chick Webb and His Orchestra, she looked like a different person. Her hair was styled, and she wore stage makeup and a pretty new evening gown.

Not only did Ella look the part of a lead vocalist, but she sounded like one, too. She sang with power and enthusiasm, occasionally kicking the side of the bandstand in her excitement. Ella charmed the Savoy crowd with her bright personality and her clear voice.

No one was more impressed by Ella's performance than Chick Webb. While he had been quick to judge Ella at first, based only on her appearance, he realized he was lucky to have found her. He wanted to hire her as a permanent member of the band.

"I thought my singing was pretty much hollering," Ella said. "But Webb didn't."

Next Webb had to convince his managers that she was the right vocalist for the band. He took Ella to audition for Moe Gale.

Gale took one look at Ella and said, "Ah, no, Chick."

"C'mon, Gale. Give her a chance," Webb pleaded.

Webb had been wrong about Ella at first, so he knew what was running through Gale's mind. "Listen to her voice," he insisted. "Don't look at her, just listen to her voice."

Gale frowned and shook his head, but he agreed to listen. Ella sang. Ella got the job.

Ella gained confidence onstage singing with Chick Webb and His Orchestra in the 1930s. Her recordings soon climbed to the top of the music charts.

❧ SIX ❧

BEGINNINGS AND ENDINGS

By mid-1935, eighteen-year-old Ella Fitzgerald was the starring attraction of the Chick Webb band. Jazz music, especially swing, soared in popularity and dominated the music scene in the United States. Louis Armstrong warbled across the airwaves, "It Don't Mean A Thing (If It Ain't Got That Swing)," a song by another jazz great, Duke Ellington. His words could have been the theme song of the era.

In the 1930s, before the introduction of television, radio shows that featured live musical broadcasts were a popular form of entertainment. Radio also played recorded music and, as a result, strongly influenced the careers of musical artists. Radio stations kept a running toll of how many times a song played on the air in a given week. The most-played songs made the hit parade, a list of top hits published in music magazines such as *Billboard* and *Melody Maker.*

Ella, along with Chick Webb and His Orchestra, made her first vocal recording on June 12, 1935, on the Decca Records label. Decca Records had been formed in 1934 by the Decca Recording Company, one of the pioneers of early sound recording. Ella's first record featured her singing "Love and Kisses." On the flip side, Charles Linton sang "Are You Here to Stay?"

The legendary Duke Ellington composed hundreds of jazz works, including many of the classics.

In the June 1935 edition of *Metronome,* a jazz magazine, reviewer George T. Simon gave Chick Webb and His Orchestra a B+ rating. Simon added, "Miss Fitzgerald should go places."

When "Love and Kisses" was released, Ella was still a legal minor who wasn't allowed to enter a drinking establishment. One night during a promotional tour for the new record, the Webb band was in Philadelphia, Pennsylvania. Ella tried to enter a tavern to listen to her first record on the jukebox. But the bar owners wouldn't let her in.

"So," remembered Ella, "I had some fellow who was over twenty-one go in and put a nickel in while I stood outside and listened to my own voice coming out."

From the beginning of her career, critics complained that Ella was too sweet for jazz. Some said she wasn't a serious artist, like the popular singer Billie Holiday, who sang the blues, a music characterized by sad songs and strong feeling. In contrast, Ella sang in a more upbeat, lighthearted manner. Critics commented on Ella's almost childlike quality. She didn't ooze sex appeal like many female singers. She wasn't a charismatic beauty like Billie Holiday. Ella didn't rely on her sexuality to sell herself. She relied on her talent alone.

Ella had a beautiful, clear, velvety voice. "Fitzgerald simply exists in tune," wrote a music critic. "And she hits every note that there is without the slightest trace of effort." Ella had a very flexible vocal range—she could sing notes up and down the scale with perfect pitch. One observer commented, "She had a vocal range so wide you needed an elevator to go from the top to the bottom." Another journalist wrote that Ella had "a sweet, girlish voice that could leap, slide, or growl anywhere within a range of three octaves."

Critics contrasted Ella's jazz with Billie Holiday's blues. Billie (right) sang sad songs in her trademark husky voice.

    With Ella at the helm, the Chick Webb band was "the perfect swing orchestra of 1936," according to Leonard Feather, music critic for the *Melody Maker* jazz review. "Amid that dark world of Lindy Hoppers [people who danced the Lindy, a type of jitterbug dance from Harlem in the 1930s], of laughter and light ale . . . of low lights and swing music," he wrote, "the arrangements of Chick Webb and his Chicks stood out like the Aurora Borealis in a sullen sky."

    Ella was also blessed with a great memory. She could easily remember the lyrics to dozens of songs, a talent that would come in handy throughout her career. At every rehearsal, Ella scribbled the song lyrics on index cards. She would sing from the cards during rehearsal, then take them home to memorize the words. Come show time, Ella was prepared.

The Chick Webb orchestra received a lot of radio play, making several live radio broadcasts in the mid-1930s. As the band soared in popularity, so did Ella. Rival bandleader Jimmie Lunceford offered her a job with his band for seventy-five dollars a week, twenty-five dollars more than she was making with Chick.

When Chick heard about Lunceford's offer, he was furious. Ella was not only his singer, but she had become his friend as well. How dare Lunceford try to recruit Ella! Chick

The Savoy Ballroom marquee announced the Jimmy [sic] *Lunceford Orchestra and the Chick Webb Orchestra in 1935.*

promptly upped her salary to one hundred twenty-five dollars a week, a good deal of money at the time. Ella stayed on with the band.

In early 1937, Chick took his band on the road, leaving Ella behind to take over the band's Savoy engagements. The Teddy Hill band, a swing orchestra, filled in for Webb and accompanied Ella.

Ella also continued to make radio appearances. In January and February 1937, she broadcast live concerts for Moe Gale's radio program, *Good Time Society.* She also recorded two songs —"Big Boy Blue" and "Dedicated to You"—with the Mills Brothers singing group. Ella was thrilled when both

Jimmie Lunceford (left) tried unsuccessfully to steal Ella away from Chick Webb's band.

songs became hits, landing on the music charts in April 1937. In November, she was voted Number One Female Vocalist in *Down Beat* and *Melody Maker* magazine polls.

Swing music was the most popular form of jazz in the 1930s and 1940s, a period known as the swing era. Musicians such as Benny Goodman, Glenn Miller, Woody Herman, Count Basie, Tommy and Jimmy Dorsey, and Artie Shaw popularized many swing tunes with their big bands.

The big bands were exactly that—large ensembles of musicians playing highly orchestrated music. Beginning in the mid-1920s, bandleaders Fletcher Henderson and Duke Ellington began using a lineup of three sax players, three brass players, and four rhythm players. By the end of the 1930s, the groups had expanded to four saxes and six brass, and by the 1940s, the big bands were even bigger, with as many as twenty musicians playing onstage at once. Swing music inspired swing dancing, a fast, fun dance form.

Glenn Miller, a trombonist and composer, was the first white big-band leader to play publicly with African American musicians. He achieved worldwide fame with tunes like "Moonlight Serenade" and was crowned "King of Swing."

As the very danceable swing music grew in popularity, many performers wanted in on the sensation. People who usually sang different kinds of music, such as country or folk, experimented with swing jazz. Country singer Stuff Smith "swang" on his fiddle. And Maxine Sullivan, a New York-based singer, even put swing into folk music.

Ella had fun experimenting with swing. One day in 1939, she hummed "A-Tisket, A-Tasket," a nursery rhyme she used to sing as a child. Ella had an inspiration. Why not put an up-tempo beat on the rhyme and make it swing? The result was fantastic. Ella soon had her first composition, and a hit song.

THE KING OF JAZZ

Ella Fitzgerald was known as the First Lady of Jazz. And her friend, trumpet player and singer Louis Armstrong, reigned as the King of Jazz. Daniel Louis Armstrong was born on August 4, 1901, to Willie and Mayanne Armstrong. The family lived in Back O' Town, one of the poorest sections of New Orleans, Louisiana. When Louis was a baby, his father abandoned the family. Mayanne put Louis and his sister Beatrice in the care of her mother-in-law, Josephine Armstrong.

As a boy, Louis helped support his family by singing on street corners. He bought his first instrument, a cornet, at the age of six.

His life took a fateful turn when he was eleven. During a New Year's Eve celebration, Louis fired a pistol into the air. The New Orleans juvenile court sent him to the Colored Waif's Home for Boys.

At the children's home, Louis received his first music lessons. He also played in the Waif's Home's brass band. He later said of the experience, "Me and music got married at the home."

When Louis was released in June 1914, he considered himself a musician. Just twelve years old, he earned money by singing with a barbershop quartet on street corners and playing music on the riverboats that sailed the Mississippi River. When he was seventeen, Louis met the man who became his mentor, Joe "King" Oliver. King and other musicians, including Jelly Roll Morton, were playing a new kind of music, a mixture of ragtime music and blues. Louis began performing with King and his band in small New Orleans jazz clubs.

In the early 1920s, jazz music was catching on in the United States, especially in the big jazz centers of New Orleans, Chicago, and New York. In 1922 Armstrong thought he would try his luck in Chicago, where he joined King Oliver's Creole Jazz Band, a

Dixieland jazz band. Louis's first recorded solo performance was on the band's 1923 recording "Chimes Blues." In 1924 Louis left Oliver to join the Fletcher Henderson Orchestra in New York City, impressing the band with his talent for improvisation.

Over the next few years, Armstrong traveled back and forth between Chicago and New York, playing with a variety of bands. In Chicago in 1926, he recorded "Cornet Chop Suey" and "Heebie Jeebies," in which he first sang scat, a rhythmic, wordless singing. With scat, he could make his voice sound like a trumpet. Although some critics said that scat singing was invented years earlier by an unknown jazz artist, Armstrong brought scat into the musical mainstream. He also revolutionized jazz by highlighting solo performances within a band and by helping invent swing music.

In the years to follow, Louis recorded hits including "Potato Head Blues" (1927), "Struttin' with Some Barbecue" (1927), "Hotter than That" (1927), "Tight Like This" (1928), "West End Blues" (1928), and a duet with pianist Earl Hines, "Weather Bird" (1928). Louis returned to New York City in 1929, headlining at Connie's Inn, a popular Harlem nightclub, and was featured in a Broadway play, *Hot Chocolates*. By this time, jazz music had gained worldwide popularity, and Armstrong was known as the fun-loving, big-hearted King of Jazz. He acquired the nickname "Satchmo" in the early 1930s, during the first of many European tours. London fans nicknamed him "Satchel mouth" (later just Satchmo) because of the way his cheeks puffed out when he played his trumpet.

Throughout the 1930s and 1940s, Armstrong recorded music with many of the big jazz stars, including Ella Fitzgerald. He appeared in a movie for the first time in 1936, in *Pennies From Heaven*. As swing music faded in popularity in the 1940s, Louis formed smaller bands and shined as a trumpeter. He and his band, the All Stars, produced many hit records, including *Louis Armstrong and the All Stars at Symphony Hall, Louis Armstrong and the All Stars at the Crescendo,* and *Louis Armstrong Plays W. C. Handy*. In 1959 Louis was on tour with the All Stars when he had his first heart attack. He recovered and continued to tour and play the music he loved until his death on July 6, 1971.

In a 1970 recording of his classic song "What a Wonderful World," Louis Armstrong sings that it would be a wonderful world if we would all give love a chance. These lyrics sum up the philosophy of one of the most talented, innovative, and beloved jazz musicians in history.

"A-Tisket, A-Tasket," recorded by Decca Records, landed at the top of the record charts almost immediately and stayed on the hit parade, a list of hit songs, for nineteen weeks. The song's huge success moved Ella's career forward at lightning speed.

People all over the country were listening to Ella on the radio, buying her records, and dancing to her tunes in jukebox joints. Ella, who had been homeless and broke just five years earlier, was a star. She tried not to think about her growing fame. It made her nervous. Despite her success, she often felt unsure of herself and shy. She comforted herself with food, but that made her gain weight, which only made her feel worse. She tried not to worry about her fame and instead focused on what she felt comfortable with—singing.

In early 1939, Ella and the Chick Webb band recorded several songs, including the swing hits "Tain't What You Do (It's the Way That Cha Do It)" and "Chew, Chew, Chew, Chew Your Bubble Gum." The band traveled frequently to perform their music in towns around the country.

Just before an upcoming tour of the southern states in May 1939, Chick Webb's lifelong spinal disease suddenly worsened. His doctor recommended immediate surgery.

Chick knew the surgery was risky. He could die. But instead of being worried about himself, he was concerned for Ella. He thought of her almost as a daughter. "[If] anything happens to me . . . take care of Ella," Chick told musician friend Teddy McRae.

"Ah, man, come on. You're going to be all right," McRae tried to reassure Webb. "You know everything's going to be all right."

"Just take care of Ella," Chick said.

While Chick was recovering in the hospital, Ella and the

band hit the road in their tour bus. They had an exhausting schedule, performing in a new city every night.

One night in mid-June, the band started a new gig in Alabama. They had been on the road all day, and when they got off the bus they hurried to the ballroom where they were performing. Strangely, from the moment the band started playing, the Alabama audience didn't make a sound. "Nobody clapped or nothing," said band member McRae. "Everybody just stood there and looked at us."

After the show, the band found out why the audience was so quiet—Chick Webb had died earlier that day. The Alabama

Thousands of mourners gathered outside the Waters African Methodist Church in Baltimore, Maryland, for Chick Webb's funeral.

crowd had learned of Webb's death on the radio. Since Ella and the band had been on the bus all day, they hadn't heard the news.

Chick died in his mother's arms, surrounded by family and friends. Just before he died, he asked his mother to lift his head so that he could see everyone in the room. "I'm sorry, but I gotta go!" he announced as he died.

Silent with grief, Ella and the band stopped their tour and headed north for Chick's funeral in his hometown, Baltimore, Maryland. Because thousands of people showed up for the funeral, the police had to stop traffic all across the city. At the funeral service, Ella sang a tribute to Chick Webb, a song called "My Buddy," a sad jazz song about losing a loyal friend.

Music writer Leonard Feather reported, "At Chick's funeral, Ella's voice achieved a poignant beauty it could never surpass." Ella had special feelings for Chick. He had helped her so much, personally and professionally. "He was always in pain, but no one ever knew it," she said. "If he'd have taken the same time that he applied to helping people, and rested, he'd have lived longer than his twenty-nine years."

A couple of weeks after the death of Chick Webb, Ella was back to work, just as Chick would have wanted. She took over the role of bandleader, and the newly named Ella Fitzgerald and Her Famous Orchestra returned to the recording studio. On June 29, 1939, they cut several songs, including, "I Want the Waiter (with the Water)."

The band's popularity increased steadily. Ella and the musicians developed a new act, billing themselves as Ella Fitzgerald and the Famous Chick Webb Orchestra. Once again they hit the road, visiting theaters and dance halls in towns up and down the East Coast, traveling everywhere by bus.

In 1939 buses did not have rest rooms or air conditioning. The traveling was hard on the band. Ella had to stay on the bus for long stretches of time and sometimes even get dressed on the bus. "It was really rough on a girl traveling with a band, especially in the summertime," said Teddy McRae.

When Ella wasn't touring with the band, she spent long days in rehearsal or in the recording studio. She was so busy working, she almost forgot to have a private life.

"No one worked as hard as she did," said John McDonough, a musician who worked with Ella. "It didn't make any difference about days off, holidays, or how many shows in one day. It made no difference whether it was Detroit or Iowa. . . . Her life revolved around the stage."

Eventually, Ella did venture out. She noticed one particular man who showed up at all of her performances. While Ella had plenty of regulars, fans who came to every show, this man was different. He stared at Ella with a longing gaze, and he asked her out on a date. His name was Benjamin Kornegay.

Ella hadn't dated many men in her life. She was flattered by Ben's interest in her, and she liked the attention. Ella let Ben into her life. She spent all of her free time with him, and he traveled with Ella and the band in the tour bus. At age twenty-four, Ella was in love for the first time.

On Friday, December 26, 1941, Ella and Benjamin were married in St. Louis, Missouri. While Ella adored Ben and told the press of her "wedded bliss," others were suspicious of him.

On several occasions, money that the band had earned on the road "disappeared." Members of the band suspected

Ella in the 1940s

Kornegay of taking the money, but Ella would hear nothing of it. She trusted her husband.

Other times, Ben reported that he had lost money. Ella would fill his pockets again, never suspecting a thing. Meanwhile, her husband grew more involved in her career and her finances.

Manager Moe Gale was concerned. Soon after Ella's marriage, Gale hired a private investigator to check out Kornegay's past. The results of the investigation were alarming. Kornegay had a criminal record. He had been a petty thief and had served time on drug charges in the 1930s. He had never told Ella about his past.

Gale was upset and tried to warn Ella. He told her about Ben Kornegay's criminal history and said he was certain Kornegay had married her for her money. At first Ella refused to believe Gale. She clung to the idea that her husband really loved her. But a few months later, Ella's common sense took hold, and she filed for divorce.

Kornegay didn't want a divorce, and he hired lawyers to fight back. Moe Gale hired lawyers for Ella, who eventually proved that the marriage was motivated by criminal intent.

Ella's divorce was finalized just six months after her wedding. The judge in the case tried to make light of the grim event. "You go back to singing 'A-Tisket, A-Tasket' and leave the boys alone," he reportedly told Ella.

Ella and legendary trumpet player Dizzy Gillespie (right) *recorded several songs together.*

✂ SEVEN ✂

LADY BE GOOD

Nineteen forty-two proved to be a busy year for Ella. In March, she sang her hit "A-Tisket, A-Tasket" in the feature film *Ride 'Em Cowboy,* starring the comedy duo Bud Abbott and Lou Costello. She also continued to tour steadily. Meanwhile, the guys in the band, one by one, were drafted into military service. The United States had entered World War II in December 1941, after the Japanese bombing of Pearl Harbor, Hawaii. The United States joined the Allied powers—France, Great Britain, and Russia—to fight Germany, Japan, and Italy in a deadly conflict that involved most of the world.

For the first time in her career, Ella teamed up with another band, a trio called the Three Keys. Ella recorded a hit record, *All I Need Is You,* with the Three Keys before they, too, were drafted. Ella's career then took another direction.

Ella never hesitated to try new singing techniques and

Saxophonist Charlie "Bird" Parker played bebop-style jazz.

styles. She loved the challenge of learning cutting-edge material. In the early 1940s, she was especially eager to sing the emerging jazz style known as bebop.

Bebop, also called bop, was developed by the brilliant trumpet player Dizzy Gillespie, saxophonist Charlie Parker (nicknamed "Bird"), and others. Known for its fast, irregular rhythms, bebop featured a return to a smaller band of four or five players, as in the original jazz bands. Bebop bands included only one instrument of a kind, such as a trumpet, saxophone, horn, and drums, rather than the large instrumental sections used by big bands and swing bands.

Dizzy Gillespie was a talented jazz trumpeter, composer, and bandleader. He was known as one of the original pioneers of bop music and scat singing. Scat is the art of singing improvised nonsense syllables, as in Gillespie's songs "Oop-Pop-a-Da" and "Oo-Bop-Sh'Bam-a-Klook-a-Mop." Gillespie played with many bands throughout his career. In the early 1940s, he teamed up with Cab Calloway's big band. He also worked with Ella for a while.

Ella learned to scat from Dizzy. She could make her voice sound like a trumpet, a saxophone, and even a trombone. "I just tried to do what I heard the horns in the band doing," she said.

The recording of the hits "Flying Home" in 1945 and "Lady Be Good" in 1947 established Ella's reputation as a top-of-the-line scat singer. "No one before Miss Fitzgerald employed the [scat] technique with such dazzling inventiveness," one writer noted.

Singer Mel Tormé remembered hearing Ella's "Lady Be Good" for the first time: "My manager at the time called me one night around 11:00 and said, 'Mel, I know it's late, but you have got to come down to my office. You've got to hear a new record.' He played me Ella's 'Lady Be Good' . . . [and I listened to the song] over and over and over again. I had never heard music like it before."

Tormé was so moved by the record that he himself began to scat—and eventually became famous for it. But he gave Ella credit for showing him and many others how to do it. "We all leaned on her," he said. "We all said, 'Okay, we're following in your footsteps. You lead us on.'"

Aside from the fun of learning to scat, Ella had another

reason to hang out with Dizzy Gillespie. She had taken a liking to Dizzy's bass player, Ray Brown. Brown, born in Pittsburgh, Pennsylvania, in 1926, was nine years younger than Ella. Ella and Ray started dating in 1947. She often came to see Ray perform in Dizzy's shows.

On December 10, 1947, Ella and Ray Brown were married in Ohio. Upon their return to New York, the newlyweds rented an apartment on Ditmars Boulevard in Queens, a borough of the city. Shortly after the marriage, Ella's half-sister,

Singer Mel Tormé gave Ella credit for teaching him how to scat.

Frances, contacted Ella and Ray. Frances was having personal problems and was unable to care for her two-year-old son. Without hesitation, Ella and Ray adopted the boy, whom they called Ray Jr. Because of Ella and Ray's full work schedules, a nanny often cared for the boy.

Ray, Dizzy, and the band had an important gig with a touring concert series called Jazz at the Philharmonic (JATP). This landmark jazz program, named for the auditorium in Los Angeles where the concerts were first held, had been launched in 1945 by an ambitious talent manager named Norman Granz. By 1948 Granz had built JATP into a successful touring series, playing to sellout crowds in cities across the United States.

One night at one of Dizzy's JATP concerts, fans spotted Ella sitting in the audience. They begged her to sing. She bashfully agreed. Norman Granz watched from the wings. Granz, who managed such major talents as Billie Holiday and Duke Ellington, was impressed. In fact, he thought that Ella might be one of the greatest jazz singers of all. He also knew that although she was popular, she didn't have a strong business manager. Granz wanted to be her manager. He wanted to make her rich—and fatten his own pocketbook along the way. Granz offered Ella a contract, and she accepted.

Granz was constantly thinking of new ways to promote Ella's career. He propelled her to a new level of success. Instead of limiting her performances to dance halls and nightclubs, he booked engagements for her at classy concert halls and posh night spots, such as Carnegie Hall and the Copacabana in New York City. In 1949 Ella performed on one of the first jazz programs broadcast on the new medium of television, on a show hosted by singer Eddie Condon.

Some of Ella's associates thought that Granz had too

much control over Ella and her career. But Norman had his own viewpoint. "[Ella] was . . . alive on this earth to make music. Her head was filled with songs," he said. "She was, however, almost entirely unable to negotiate the real world—the airline ticket-buying, hotel reservation-making, letter-mailing, doctor-calling, taxi-hailing, musician-firing, contract-reading, dress-altering, interview-giving, wide, wide world of human habitation."

Granz handled all of those details for Ella and kept her busy with performances. On September 18, 1949, Ella appeared at a JATP concert at Carnegie Hall, along with jazz greats Charlie Parker and Lester Young, a sax player. Granz had arranged for another eminent jazz figure to appear onstage as well—the Canadian jazz pianist Oscar Peterson. During the concert, Peterson, who was planted in the audience by Granz, was beckoned onstage to perform. The crowd loved him, and Peterson's "spontaneous" performance earned him a job on the JATP tour.

Granz made both Peterson and Ella (and many others) into internationally famous artists. In addition to scheduling performances for Ella in theaters all over the country, he arranged for her to record for Decca Records.

Granz encouraged Ella to take her natural singing abilities to the limit. He wanted her to sing many kinds of music besides jazz. "Norman forced her to see herself in a much truer context by asking her to do things she didn't want to do," said Oscar Peterson. "Then, after she did them, she'd come back and she was glad he made her do it."

Granz didn't spare costs when it came to pampering his clients. Once he gave Ella a new fur coat. Oscar Peterson decided to play a joke on Ella, who prized her new coat. He bought a bottle of trick ink (an ink bottle that comes with a

Ella around 1950

plastic "inkblot" that the trickster places by the bottle) and visited Ella in her dressing room. Before she left to go onstage, Oscar made sure that Ella saw him writing with the ink pen.

Ella warned Oscar to be careful with his pen since her new coat was lying nearby. Oscar assured Ella that nothing was going to happen to her coat. But as soon as she left the room, he turned the ink bottle over and put the fake inkblot on her fur coat.

When Ella returned, Oscar pretended to be crying. He told her that he couldn't believe what had happened.

Ella asked him what was the matter. She didn't see anything wrong with her coat. Then she looked and saw the ink "spill," and her eyes filled with tears.

But Ella wasn't crying about her fur coat. She tried to smile and to assure Oscar that it was okay. She told him not to worry about the accident—she just hated to see him cry.

Oscar Peterson remembered the incident well. "She was more concerned about me than the coat. She was . . . such a sweet person."

Onstage, Ella always seemed to be having a great time. But under the confident surface, she often suffered stage fright. Offstage, she was shy, insecure, and reserved, even with her best friends.

Musician Charles Linton knew Ella well in her early days as a singer. He recalled one of the many subway trips he took with Ella, from downtown New York to Harlem. "[When people looked at her] she was self-conscious, you know, because her hair was real short. . . . If someone turned to look at her and turned to one of their friends and said something, that was it, kid! Oh! That was it! I'd say, They're not saying anything. You're a star now. They're saying, 'I saw her at the

Savoy Ballroom. I saw her at the Apollo Theater.' But that didn't change anything, she was so conscious of herself."

Music critic Jay Cocks once contrasted Ella with Billie Holiday. "Billie Holiday's music was a lifeline. She lived out all the suffering of her songs. For Ella, music seemed more like a safe harbor, a home from which she rarely ventured."

Ella rehearsing for a jazz concert in Stockholm, Sweden, in 1952. Oscar Peterson (foreground), *Roy Eldridge* (right), *and Max Roach* (background) *accompanied her.*

❧ EIGHT ❧

THE SONGBOOKS

In 1951 Ray Brown began touring with the Oscar Peterson Trio. Ella often accompanied her husband on the road. Many times during the long haul cross-country by bus, the band members amused themselves by playing music for each other. The guys would grab their instruments from the back of the bus and start jamming, playing spontaneously just for fun. Usually Ella would sing along.

One day Ella surprised everyone in the band. "[She] pulled out a harmonica," said Oscar Peterson, "and wasted everybody. She really did! She has that kind of talent, believe me. It's a special talent, and those who have not been fortunate enough to play for her would not realize how deeply God gifted her."

Ella and Ray both worked hard at their careers. Ray was often on the road, and sometimes Ella didn't see him for weeks. When Ray was home, Ella was working or was on tour herself. Their marriage began to fall apart.

In August 1953, Ella and Ray divorced. The end of their marriage was not bitter—they remained friends afterward. They shared custody of Ray Jr. and continued to perform the music they loved.

Norman Granz continued to encourage Ella to sing new material and expand her repertoire. "Norman felt that I should do other things," Ella said, "so he produced the *Cole Porter Songbook* with me. It was a turning point in my life."

Under Granz's direction, Ella produced a series of songbook albums that featured the works of several popular American composers, including Cole Porter, Duke Ellington, Irving Berlin, and George and Ira Gershwin. The first songbook, featuring Cole Porter compositions, was recorded in February 1956 and included "Miss Otis Regrets," "Anything Goes," "From This Moment On," and other memorable numbers. Throughout the 1950s, Ella worked on the songbooks, creating timeless tributes to great composers.

Critics and composers alike praised Ella's renditions of the classic American songs. Her rich voice and perfect intonation was particularly well suited for ballads, such as "Where or When" or "Ev'rytime We Say Goodbye." One writer commented, "Play an Ella ballad with a cat in the room, and the animal will invariably go up to the speaker, lie down and purr."

While Ella shined as a celebrity, racist attitudes in the United States clouded her success. On a Pan-American Airlines flight to Australia for a concert date, Ella and her African American band members were bumped from the flight during a layover in Hawaii, and the airline gave their seats to white passengers. Unable to schedule another flight in time, Ella was forced to cancel the Australian concert.

Ella began singing and recording the songs of Ira (left) *and George Gershwin* (right) *in the 1950s.*

Granz was furious. He promptly brought a racial discrimination lawsuit against the airline. The case was eventually settled out of court (the airline paid Ella and the band an undisclosed amount of money). Antidiscrimination laws were not yet in place in the United States, but Ella and Granz's efforts to fight back made significant strides toward social change.

Ella and other black musicians most commonly faced racism when they attempted to book concerts in ritzy clubs with a white clientele. To help combat the racism in such clubs, the famous movie star Marilyn Monroe used the power of her fame. Marilyn had first seen Ella perform in 1954 in a nightclub near Marilyn's Hollywood home. She had fallen in love with Ella's singing.

*Ella chatted with friend and supporter Marilyn Monroe at a jazz
session in Hollywood.*

Norman Granz and Marilyn Monroe persuaded Charlie
Morrison, the owner of Hollywood's upscale Mocambo nightclub, to open his doors for the first time to a black singer—
Ella. Morrison reluctantly agreed. Marilyn was a powerful
person in Hollywood, and Morrison couldn't afford to make
her mad.

On Ella's opening night at the Mocambo, Marilyn planted
some of her famous friends in the audience, celebrities like
Frank Sinatra and Judy Garland. The show was a tremendous
success, and Morrison asked Ella to return. Each night, she
sang to a full house.

Ella's triumph at the Mocambo opened doors, not only for herself, but for other black performers as well. Norman booked her for an engagement at the elegant Venetian Room in San Francisco's Fairmont Hotel. Ella was the first black singer to perform at the hotel.

In 1956 Ella appeared at the Hollywood Bowl, a club in Los Angeles, accompanied by the JATP rhythm section. Again, she wowed the crowd with her sizzling, swinging

The famous Mocambo nightclub in Hollywood

Ella joined fellow singer Frank Sinatra (left) *on the* Frank Sinatra-Timex Show *in the late 1950s.*

rhythm and outstanding voice. One spectator commented, "Ella Fitzgerald could sing the Van Nuys [California] telephone directory with a broken jaw and make it sound good—and that's a particularly dull telephone directory."

In January 1957, Ella performed at New York's Paramount Theatre with the smooth-voiced popular singer Nat "King" Cole and Count Basie and his orchestra. During the concert, Ella was overcome with agonizing stomach pain and was rushed to the hospital. Doctors found an abdominal abscess and operated immediately.

Ella was determined to get back on her feet and return to work. At the end of March, she appeared on *The Ed Sullivan Show,* a popular TV variety program. In great spirits, she sang "Thanks for the Memory."

Later in 1957, Ella decided to move to Los Angeles. There she could enjoy the sunshine and be close to her business manager, Norman Granz. Ella bought a big house set back from the road, at 3971 Hepburn Avenue in Beverly Hills.

"I decorated the new house myself," Ella said in a 1957

Ella performed with Oscar Moore (left), *Wesley Prince* (center), *and Nat "King" Cole* (right) *in 1957. The King Cole Trio recorded countless jazz classics.*

interview. "I'd sure like to . . . spend more time with Ray, Jr. I don't think I'd ever give up the tours though. Being on the road gets rough sometimes, but I'd sure miss singing to the people."

Although Ella was basically a very shy person, she loved to perform. She wanted more than anything to please her audiences and be accepted by them. But despite her many fans and admirers, Ella was lonely. She didn't get close to people easily. "I want to get married again," she told a reporter for the *New York Mirror.* "I'm still looking. Everybody needs companionship."

Ella continued to challenge herself musically. When she added show tunes to her act, she proved that a song from a Broadway musical could stand alone, outside of the context of the play. Ella's 1958 interpretation of "I Loves You Porgy," from the musical *Porgy and Bess* by the prolific songwriting duo George and Ira Gershwin, stood out from previous versions.

In 1959 Ella recorded a five-album set, *Ella Fitzgerald Sings the George and Ira Gershwin Songbook,* with Nelson Riddle as musical director. The record included the hit compositions "Nice Work If You Can Get It," "'S Wonderful," and "The Man I Love."

Pianist Lou Levy remembered the grueling weeks in the recording studio working on the lengthy Gershwin songbook with Ella. "Ella would come in and sing with her hand over her ear in that little isolation booth . . . and we would just crank them out, one after the other. Funny thing, they never sounded as if they were cranked out."

For two years following the release of the Gershwin songbook, Ella topped *Down Beat* and *Metronome* magazines' music polls and won the *Down Beat* critics' award. "I never knew

Nelson Riddle and Ella worked together on classic recordings of George and Ira Gershwin songs.

how good our songs were until I heard Ella Fitzgerald sing them," said Ira Gershwin, who wrote the lyrics to the music composed by his brother George.

"She sings the Gershwins sublimely," wrote a music critic, "because they were as drawn to high spirits and perpetual youth as she."

With Ella's fame at an all-time high, Norman Granz knew the time was ripe for her to take her talents abroad. He arranged her first European tour in 1960. The concerts would be recorded for Verve Records, a company Norman had started in 1956. These live concerts in cities such as Rome, Italy, and West Berlin would be preserved forever for her fans.

European audiences loved Ella. In Italy, children called her "Mama Jazz." "I thought that was so cute. As long as they don't call me Grandma Jazz," Ella joked.

Ella's concert in Berlin was a special success. Ella and her band—Paul Smith on piano, Jim Hall on guitar, Wilfred Middlebrooks on bass, and Gus Johnson on drums—performed with gusto and energy, charged up by the twelve thousand fans who filled Berlin's Deutschlandhalle concert hall. She performed several favorites, including "The Man I Love," "Summertime," and "That Old Black Magic," but the highlight of the concert was her rendition of "Mack the Knife."

"It was the first version and the best, where she got kind of loused up with the lyrics, which was the charm of the thing," recalled pianist Paul Smith. "She could always ad-lib her way out of anything, and that was the hook that got that record off the ground!"

During the song, Ella forgot some of the words, so she winged it by singing, "Oh, what's the next chorus to this song now/This is the one now I don't know." She made fun of herself, singing, "And now Ella Ella and her fellas/We're making a wreck, what a wreck of Mack the Knife."

Ella was at her most creative when performing live. While singing "Mack the Knife" in Berlin, she amused the crowd by mimicking one of her favorite singers and friends, Louis Armstrong. She captured Armstrong's distinctive deep, gravelly voice.

Mack the Knife: Ella in Berlin became an all-time favorite recording. It won two Grammy awards, for Best Vocal Performance–Female and for Best Vocal Performance Album–Female.

Ella liked to ad-lib while singing, whether she was mocking other singers or spontaneously making up lyrics. "Ella does that even on shows," recalled a musician who worked with her for many years. If there was a heckler in the crowd— an obnoxious audience member yelling out rude comments— Ella would simply sing a "swinging warning to him in the middle of a number," said the musician. If the microphone

Ella's performances in Germany helped boost her international reputation as a world-class jazz singer.

wasn't working properly, "[she'd] tell the engineer about it in words in music."

While Ella was confident onstage, before a show she was terribly nervous. "We could be at an afternoon concert playing to a small house in Mannheim, Germany, in the fifth week of a tour, doing the same show she's done every day—and she'll come backstage afterward and say, 'Do you think I did all right? I was so scared out there!'" recalled a musician who toured with her.

Ella always kept her ears open for new tunes to sing. Another musician who traveled with her remembered hearing her call out to her road manager, Pete Cavallo: "'Pete, Pete!' She'd heard a song she liked. 'Pete, get the name of that. Write that down. I want it.' We added so many songs to the book that we never got a chance to do them all."

On tour in the 1950s and 1960s, Ella also recorded live albums in Rome and Stockholm, Sweden. "On these disks the great happiness rises up like steam," said a writer for the *New York Times*. "Ella is as thrilled as we are to hear what she is singing. She is delighted, occasionally close to euphoric. She laughs. She giggles. She is a little girl, appreciating her own gifted self."

Another reviewer described Ella in 1951 as a "large cheerful child. Her smile is as entrancing as her cherubic face; her eyes twinkle with more than a touch of mischief."

Ella performed forty-three European tours during her career, sometimes two or three a year. During one European tour, Ella and the band did three weeks of one-nighters, performing in a new city each night, often two shows a night. While some of the musicians grew exhausted and sick from the workload, Ella worked tirelessly.

Musician Keter Betts remembered Ella's endless energy.

Each morning, the band members had to report to the hotel lobby at 7:45 A.M., a terribly early hour for musicians who had worked late into the night. But when Betts arrived in the lobby, he said, "Ella was already down there—fresh, sitting and singing to herself, getting ready to go to the next town."

Ella toured the world beginning in the 1950s. She performed in 1969 in Antibes, France, at the International Jazz Festival.

✂ NINE ✃

"EV'RYTIME WE SAY GOODBYE"

As Ella grew older, she didn't close her mind to the latest musical trends. "If you don't learn new songs, you're lost," she said in 1967, when she was fifty years old. "No matter where we play, we have some of the younger generation coming to the club. It's a drag if you don't have anything to offer them."

Ella was a creator as well as a vocalist. She liked to sing "songs that present some kind of a challenge and make you say to yourself, 'What are you gonna do with this?'"

Throughout her career, Ella performed a terrifically wide range of material. In the 1960s, Ella produced a pop Christmas album. She sang gospel and blues. She experimented with West Indian calypso music and Brazilian bossa nova. She even recorded a songbook of the Beatles' music.

In concert, Ella could be flexible and fun. She might

surprise the crowd by singing an old jazz standard like "Lady Be Good" and then turn around and sing the theme song from TV's *The Love Boat.*

In the 1970s, Ella made a series of television commercials for Memorex, a manufacturer of recording tape. In the classic commercials, a voice asks, "Is it live or is it Memorex?" Then a Memorex tape recording of Ella's voice shatters a wine glass. Ella earned more than one million dollars sponsoring Memorex. For nearly two decades, she was known to many American children as "the lady that breaks those glasses!"

Ella continued to sing with old friends throughout the 1970s and 1980s. Frank Sinatra (left), Ella, and Count Basie (right) came together onstage at Caesars Palace in Las Vegas, Nevada.

Jazz legends Sarah Vaughan (left) *and Pearl Bailey* (center) *harmonized with Ella in 1979 in Palm Springs, California.*

As Ella pushed herself professionally, she stressed her body to the limit. For Ella, the needs of other people—her fans, business managers, and fellow musicians—had always come first. Her own needs came last. Eventually, the stress of constant work caught up with her. Her health began to suffer and grow steadily worse. She developed diabetes, a disease of the endocrine system. Diabetes, in addition to Ella's lifelong weight problem, caused heart trouble, poor circulation, and cataracts (an eye condition that can cause blindness).

Physical exhaustion led Ella to cancel concerts on several occasions. In 1971 she had to cancel one of her European tours to have a second cataract operation. After the surgery, her doctors told her to stay home and rest. But Ella hated to sit around doing nothing. While she recovered, she studied Portuguese. She figured, "When I do those Brazilian songs I'll know what I'm singing about!"

Despite failing eyesight and physical pain, Ella kept singing. Sometimes before a concert, she felt too exhausted to perform. But once she was onstage, her energy returned.

When Ella entered her seventies, some critics said that she should retire because she was no longer "at her peak." But most fans disagreed. "I think that people who say Ella or Frank Sinatra should hang it up are totally foolish . . . we still have a lot to learn from the vantage point age and experience have brought them," argued one fan. "I'd rather hear Ella Fitzgerald not at her peak than ten other singers at their peak."

In June 1986, Ella opened the JVC Jazz Festival (formerly known as the Newport Jazz Festival) in New York. Soon after, her health took a turn for the worse. In September 1986, Ella had open-heart surgery. Afterward, she took a nine-month break to recuperate from the operation—the longest break she'd ever had.

Ella made her last commercial recording, an album called *All That Jazz,* in 1989. In the fall of 1992, Ella gave her last public concert, in West Palm Beach, Florida. At age seventy-five, Ella was ready to retire.

In her retirement, Ella lived a secluded, private life, but she kept in touch with a small circle of her good friends, including singers Sarah Vaughan and Peggy Lee. And Ella loved spending time with her granddaughter, Alice, Ray Jr.'s daughter.

Singer Mel Tormé lived a few blocks from Ella. "I adore Ella," he said. "Every time we see each other, there's a lot of hugging and kissing. . . . But I don't really know her very well. . . . I'm not sure if anybody does."

Ella's comfortable Beverly Hills home was filled with the treasures of her lifetime. A large color picture of manager Norman Granz and a photograph of her friend Marilyn Monroe decorated her living room wall. Photos of Ella at various recording sessions reminded her of good times with musician friends.

Many awards from a long career adorned Ella's house. She was proud of her thirteen Grammy awards—more than any other female vocalist in Grammy history had received.

Even as she grew older, Ella sang with style and energy. She is shown here in 1990.

Ella especially treasured her Lifetime Achievement Grammy award, presented to her in 1967.

For eighteen years in a row, Ella was named "Top Female Vocal Jazz Singer" by *Down Beat* magazine. In 1979 she was honored at the Kennedy Center in Washington, D.C., for her legendary accomplishments in music. She also received honorary music degrees from several universities, including Dartmouth and Yale. She received the Whitney Young Award from the Urban League for her contributions to the African American community. The Society of Singers named an award after her—the Ella. And in 1985, President Ronald Reagan presented Ella with the National Medal of Arts.

But Ella's biggest accomplishment was the music she made, whether she was performing in a funky Harlem jazz club or Carnegie Hall (where she appeared twenty-six times), and on the more than two hundred top-selling albums she recorded. Her music is what earned her the title "First Lady of Song."

In her later years, Ella expressed gratitude for the arrival of compact discs. The reissue of her life's work on CDs introduced a new generation of young people to Ella's work, as did renewed enthusiasm for swing music in many dance clubs.

"Coming through the years, and finding that I not only have just the fans of my day, but the young ones of today, it means it was worth all of it," she said.

On June 15, 1996, at the age of seventy-nine, Ella Jane Fitzgerald died in her Los Angeles home of complications from diabetes. Ella came into the world with many obstacles in her path. But no matter how difficult the circumstances, she trusted that things would get better. And she didn't let the bad times make her angry and bitter. "She has endured discrimination with dignity and given herself equally to black and white audiences, who in turn have taken her into their hearts," said one writer. Ella's singing filled her with joy and energy, especially because she could share her gift and make people happy.

And through her music, that gift lives on. As one young fan wrote in an online tribute to Ella, "Most of my friends listen primarily to punk and heavy metal music, like me, and

Ella proudly wore her National Medal of Arts medallion around her neck. The medal was just one of many awards she garnered during her lifetime.

ELLA'S GRAMMY AWARDS

1958 Best Vocal Performance, Female, *Ella Fitzgerald Sings the Irving Berlin Songbook*

1958 Best Jazz Performance, Individual, *Ella Fitzgerald Sings the Duke Ellington Songbook*

1959 Best Vocal Performance, Female, "But Not for Me"

1959 Best Jazz Performance, Soloist, *Ella Swings Lightly*

1960 Best Vocal Performance, Single Record or Track, Female, "Mack the Knife"

1960 Best Vocal Performance, Album, Female, *Mack the Knife: Ella in Berlin*

1962 Best Solo Vocal Performance, Female, *Ella Swings Brightly with Nelson Riddle*

1976 Best Jazz Vocal Performance, *Fitzgerald and Pass Again*

1979 Best Jazz Vocal Performance, *Fine and Mellow*

1980 Best Jazz Vocal Performance, Female, *A Perfect Match: Ella and Basie*

1981 Best Jazz Vocal Performance, Female, *Digital III at Montreux*

1983 Best Jazz Vocal Performance, Female, *The Best Is Yet to Come*

1990 Best Jazz Vocal Performance, Female, *All That Jazz*

have no interest in jazz, but I have never played Ella Fitzgerald for anyone who didn't rush right out and buy her CDs, and listen to them incessantly." Through her recordings, Ella's voice lives on.

Timeline

1917	Ella is born in Newport News, Virginia.
1921	The Fitzgeralds move to Yonkers, New York.
1927–1932	Ella listens to jazz and swing music. She sings and dances at school and at the Savoy Ballroom in Harlem, New York City.
1932	Ella moves in with her Aunt Virginia and her cousin Georgiana in Harlem.
1934	Ella drops out of school and begins living on the streets.
1934	Ella wins her first singing contest at Amateur Night at the Apollo Theater in Harlem.
1935–1937	Ella sings as lead vocalist for Chick Webb and His Orchestra.
1935	Ella, singing with Chick Webb and His Orchestra, records her first song for Decca Records.
1939	Chick Webb dies. Ella tours with the Famous Chick Webb Orchestra.
1941	Ella marries Ben Kornegay. She divorces him six months later.
1947	Ella marries Ray Brown. They adopt Ray Jr.
1949	Ella performs on one of the first jazz television programs.
1953	Ella and Ray Brown get divorced.
1956–1959	Ella records the songbook albums featuring the works of Cole Porter, Duke Ellington, Irving Berlin, and George and Ira Gershwin.
1957	Ella moves to Beverly Hills in Los Angeles, California.
1958	Ella wins her first Grammy award for *Ella Fitzgerald Sings the Irving Berlin Songbook*—Best Vocal Performance, Female.
1960	Ella begins touring Europe to perform concerts and record live albums.
1960s	Ella expands her primarily jazz repertoire by recording Christmas songs, gospel, blues, pop, and calypso music.
1970s	Ella records a series of Memorex television commercials. She develops diabetes.
1985	U.S. President Ronald Reagan awards Ella the National Medal of Arts.
1990	Ella wins her thirteenth Grammy award for *All That Jazz*—Best Jazz Vocal Performance, Female.
1992	Ella retires after a fifty-eight-year singing career.
1996	Ella dies in Los Angeles of complications from diabetes.

Sources

8 Sid Colin, *Ella: The Life and Times of Ella Fitzgerald* (London: Elm Tree Books, 1986), 1.

10-11 Stuart Nicholson, *Ella Fitzgerald: A Biography of the First Lady of Jazz* (New York: Charles Scribner's Sons, 1993), 5.

15 Jay Cocks, "The Voice of America," *Time,* June 24, 1996, 83.

15 Nicholson, 5.

15 Ibid., 7.

20 Ibid.

21 Ibid., 14.

23 Ibid.

27-28 "The Devil's Music: 1920s Jazz," *Culture Shock,* prod. and dir. María Agui Carter and Calvin A. Lindsay Jr., 60 min., Public Broadcasting Service, 2000, videocassette.

28 Ibid.

32 Nicholson, 22.

34 Colin, 14.

34 Ibid.

34 Nicholson, 21.

35 "Your Ella Fitzgerald Letters," *Redsugar's Ella Fitzgerald Page,* n.d., <http://www.redsugar.com> (n.d.).

35 Leonard G. Feather, *From Satchmo to Miles* (New York: Stein and Day, 1972), 82.

37 Nicholson, 34.

39 Ibid.

39 Ibid.

40 Ibid., 35.

40 Ibid.

41 Ibid.

41 Feather, 90.

42 Stephen Holden, "World's 'First Lady of Song' Dies at 78," © 1996 New York Times News Service, *Lexington Herald-Leader Online,* <http://www.Kentuckyconnect. com/heraldleader/news/0616/ n19ella.html> (October 4, 1996).

42 "The Greatest: Ella Fitzgerald Dies," *Virtually Northwest,* June 16, 1996, <http://www.virtuallynw. com/~vnw/stories/1996> (November 29, 1996).

43 Ibid.

47 Feather, 90.

47 Ibid.

47 Will Friedwald, "Ella: 1917–1996: A Memorial, The Decca Years, Vol. One, 1935–1938" (record liner notes), n.d., <http://www.spcc.com/ella/ decca.html> (n.d.).

47 Samantha Miller, "The First Lady of Song: Music World Remembers Ella Fitzgerald," *People Magazine Online,* June 18, 1996, <http://www.people.com> (October 4, 1996).

47 "The Greatest: Ella Fitzgerald Dies," *Virtually Northwest.*

48 Feather, 88.

48 Ibid., 87.

54 Nicholson, 61.

55 Ibid.

56 Feather, 91.

56 Colin, 54.

56 Feather, 91.

56 Colin, 55.

57 Nicholson, 70.

57 Cocks, 83.

59 Nicholson, 68.

63 Jim Moret, "Ella Fitzgerald Dies at Age 78," *Cable News Network, Inc.,* June 15, 1996, <http://www.nmis.org/ NewsInteractive/CNN/ Newsroom/A19960612/1996/ 0617/seg6.mpg> (September 9, 1996).

63 Holden.

63 Jonathan Schwartz, "The Divine Pleasures of an 'Absent Genius,'" *New York Times,* June 23, 1996, 34.

63 Mel Tormé, "Remembering Ella Fitzgerald," interview by Jeffrey Kaye, *Public Broadcasting System Online Newshour,* June 17, 1996, <http://www.pbs.org/ newshour/bb/remember/ella_ fitzgerald.html> (October 4, 1996).

65-66 Schwartz, 34.

66 John McDonough, "Tales from Ella's Fellas," *Down Beat,* September 1995, 2.

68 Ibid., 3.

71 Ibid.

72 Cocks, 81.

72 "American Legends Interviews Geoffrey Fidelman, Author of *First Lady of Song, American Legends,"* n.d. <http://www.american legends.com/ellafitzgerald/ geoffrey.html> (October 4, 1996).

76 Feather, 96.

77-78 Nicholson, 169.

78 Ibid., 171.

78 "The Greatest: Ella Fitzgerald Dies," *Virtually Northwest.*

78-79 Margo Jefferson, "A Jazz Legend and How She Grew," *New York Times Online,* June 1, 1994, <http://www.cgibin1.erols.com/ kelleher/ella.html> (December 4, 1996).

79 Nicholson, 184.

79-80 Cocks, 81.

80 Nicholson, 190.

80-81 Feather, 94.

82 Ibid., 93.

82 Nicholson, 2.

82 Schwartz, 34.

82 Friedwald, 8.

83 Keter Betts, "The First Lady's Sideman," *Washington Post,* June 23, 1996, G1.

85 Claudia Levy, " 'First Lady of Song' Ella Fitzgerald Dies: In Six-Decade Career, She Set the Standard for Jazz Vocalists," *Washington Post,* June 16, 1996, A1.

85 Leonard Feather, "Ella Today (And Yesterday Too)," *Down Beat,* March 1994, 1.

86 Betts.

88 Feather, 95.

88 Nicholson, 225.

89 Ibid., 3.

90 Moret.

91 Nicholson, 243.

93 "Your Ella Fitzgerald Letters," *Redsugar's Ella Fitzgerald Page.*

Glossary of Jazz Terms

Bebop or Bop: A form of jazz that became popular during the 1940s. Bebop evolved from swing, an earlier jazz style. Bop music rejected the highly arranged music of the big bands and instead was played with a small band, featuring solos, improvisation, and uneven rhythms. Trumpet player Dizzy Gillespie, saxophone player Charlie Parker, guitarist Joe Pass, and pianist Thelonious Monk were all important players in the bebop movement.

Big Band: A jazz ensemble made up of ten to twenty instrumentalists, such as three sax, three brass, and four rhythm players. The big band sound achieved a peak of popularity during the 1940s.

Blues: A traditional African American music that formed in the early 1900s and continued to develop throughout the twentieth century. Blues are often sung by one singer accompanied by piano or guitar. A traditional blues song has twelve bars, or lines of music, that repeat continually and uses "blue notes," which are particular notes in a scale, such as the flat third note (i.e., E flat).

Dixieland Jazz: The earliest form of jazz. The first jazz recordings were made in 1917 in New York City by the Original Dixieland Jazz Band. The band was composed of white musicians who played music they had heard performed by black artists in New Orleans. A typical Dixieland band featured a trumpet or cornet, clarinet, trombone, and a steady beat from a bass, piano, or drums. Improvisation was a key element of Dixieland jazz.

Improvisation: The art of playing music without planning or forethought. Jazz critics say that the common element of all jazz music is improvisation—no one can predict how a piece of jazz music will sound, even after multiple performances.

Ragtime: A form of music that developed in the late 1800s in the United States and influenced jazz music. Ragtime relies on the use of syncopation, in which the regular accent or beat in a piece of music is displaced by stressing the weak beat rather than the strong one. The first published rag, "Harlem Rag," appeared in 1897 and was followed by popular ragtime tunes by composers such as Scott Joplin.

Scat: Singing improvised nonsense syllables in a way that mimics the sound of an instrument

Swing music: Created in the 1930s, swing lasted into the 1940s, with a resurgence of popularity in the 1990s. Swing music, often played by big bands, has a fast, danceable beat.

Selected Bibliography

Books

Carr, Ian, Digby Fairweather, and Brian Priestley. *Jazz: The Rough Guide.* London: Rough Guides, 1995.

Colin, Sid. *Ella: The Life and Times of Ella Fitzgerald.* London: Elm Tree Books, 1986.

Feather, Leonard. *The Book of Jazz.* New York: Horizon Press, 1957.

Feather, Leonard. *From Satchmo to Miles.* New York: Stein and Day, 1972.

Gammond, Peter, ed. *The Decca Book of Jazz.* London: Frederick Muller Ltd., 1958.

Giddins, Gary. *Visions of Jazz.* New York: Oxford University Press, 1998.

Gioia, Ted. *The History of Jazz.* New York: Oxford University Press, 1997.

Haskins, James. *The Cotton Club.* New York: Random House, 1977.

King, Johnny. *What Jazz Is: An Insider's Guide to Understanding and Listening to Jazz.* New York: Walker & Co., 1997.

Lewis, David L. *When Harlem Was in Vogue.* New York: Knopf, 1981.

Nicholson, Stuart. *Ella Fitzgerald: A Biography of the First Lady of Jazz.* New York: Charles Scribner's Sons, 1993.

Placksin, Sally. *American Women in Jazz.* New York: Seaview Books, 1982.

Porter, Lewis, and Michael Ullman, with Ed Hazell. *Jazz: From Its Origins to the Present.* Englewood Cliffs, New Jersey: Prentice-Hall, Inc., 1993.

Magazine and Newspaper Articles

Balliett, Whitney. "The First Lady of Song." *New Yorker,* April 26, 1993.

Betts, Keter. "The First Lady's Sideman." *Washington Post,* June 23, 1996.

Cocks, Jay. "The Voice of America." *Time,* June 24, 1996.

Feather, Leonard. "Ella Today (And Yesterday Too)." *Down Beat,* March 1994.

Gerber, Larry. " 'First Lady of Song' Ella Fitzgerald Dies at 78." *Daily Iowan,* June 17, 1996.

Levy, Claudia. " 'First Lady of Song' Ella Fitzgerald Dies: In Six-Decade Career, She Set the Standard for Jazz Vocalists." *Washington Post,* June 16, 1996.

McDonough, John. "Tales from Ella's Fellas." *Down Beat,* September 1995.

Schwartz, Jonathan. "The Divine Pleasures of an 'Absent Genius.' " *New York Times,* June 23, 1996.

Online Sources

"American Legends Interviews Geoffrey Fidelman, Author of First Lady of Song, American Legends." n.d. <http://www.americanlegends.com/ellafitzgerald/geoffrey.html> (October 4, 1996).

"Ella Fitzgerald: April 25, 1918 - June 15, 1996." *Jazz Central Station.* n.d. <http://www.jazzcentralstation.com> (n.d.).

"Ella Fitzgerald, Great Lady. . . Grand Duchess of Jazz." n.d. <http://www.jdscomm.com/ellafeat.html> (n.d.).

"Ella's Grammy Awards." *Virtually Northwest: An Online Service of the Spokesman-Review.* n.d. <http://www.virtuallynw.com/~vnw/stories/1996/June/16/S89417.html> (n.d.).

"Fitzgerald Dies." *Telegraph Herald Online.* n.d. <http://www.thonline.com/news/th0616/stories/14933.htm> (n.d.).

Friedwald, Will. "Ella: 1917–1996: A Memorial, The Decca Years, Vol. One, 1935–1938" (record liner notes). n.d. <http://www.spcc.com/ella/decca.html> (n.d.).

"The Greatest: Ella Fitzgerald Dies." *Virtually Northwest.* June 16, 1996. <http://www.virtuallynw.com/~vnw/stories/1996/June/16/S89309.html> (November 29, 1996).

Himes, Geoffrey. "Museum Remembers Ella's Excellence." *Life Goes On.* n.d. <http://www.lifegoes.on.com/archive/071896-080196/fitzgerald/html> (n.d.).

Holden, Stephen. "World's 'First Lady of Song' Dies at 78," © 1996 New York Times News Service, *Lexington Herald-Leader Online,* <http://www.Kentuckyconnect.com/heraldleader/news/0616/n19ella.html> (October 4, 1996).

Jefferson, Margo. "A Jazz Legend and How She Grew." *New York Times Online.* June 1, 1994. <http://www.cgibin1.erols.com/kelleher/ella.html> (December 4, 1996).

"A Memorial, The Fans Remember Ella." *Jazz Central Station.* n.d. <http://wwwjazzcentralstation.com/jcs/station/musicexp/artists/ella/remember/rememb-6.html> (n.d.)

Miller, Samantha. "The First Lady of Song: Music World Remembers Ella Fitzgerald." *People Online.* June 18, 1996. <http://www.people.com> (October 4, 1996).

Moret, Jim. "Ella Fitzgerald Dies at Age 78." *Cable News Network, Inc.* June 15, 1996. <http://www.nmis.org/NewsInteractive/CNN/Newsroom/A19960612/1996/0617/seg6.mpg> (September 9, 1996).

Redsugar's Ella Fitzgerald Page. n.d. <http://www.redsugar.com> (n.d.).

"Remembering Ella Fitzgerald." *Public Broadcasting System Online Newshour.* June 17, 1996. <http://www/pbs.org/newshour/bb/remember/ella_fitzgerald.html> (October 4, 1996).

Windsor, Vernon. *Ella Fitzgerald Web Page.* n.d. <http://vwindsor@ iastate.edu> (n.d.).

Other Sources

"The Devil's Music: 1920s Jazz." *Culture Shock.* Produced and directed by María Agui Carter and Calvin A. Lindsay Jr., 60 min. Public Broadcasting Service, 2000. Videocassette.

Fayer, Steve. *The Great Depression: New Deal/New York.* Produced by Blackside, Inc., 57 min. Public Broadcasting Service, 1993. Videocassette.

Friedwald, Will. *Ella Fitzgerald, 1917-1996: A Tribute.* Written for program of a Carnegie Hall Tribute to Ella Fitzgerald, 1996. Videocassette.

Discography Highlights

Ella recorded hundreds of songs and a wealth of albums in her lifetime. Record companies continue to release new Fitzgerald CDs each year. Below is a sampling of Ella's tremendous discography. (Note that minor inconsistencies in title presentation do occur across sources. This selected discography is from the Ella Fitzgerald page of the All Music Guide website at <http://www.allmusic.com>.)

1935	*Ella Fitzgerald* (ASV/Living Era)
1938	*Ella and Her Fellas* (Decca)
1938	*75th Birthday Celebration* (GRP)
1939	*The Chick Webb Orchestra Directed by Ella Fitzgerald* (Jazz Anthology)
1940	*Ella Fitzgerald and Her Famous Orchestra* (Sunbeam)
1940	*Live from the Roseland Ballroom New York 1940* (Jazz Anthology)
1940	*New York 1940* (Jazz Anthology)
1940	*Sing Song Swing* (Laserlight)
1944	*For Sentimental Reasons* (Decca)
1945	*Lullabies of Birdland* (Decca)
1948	*Ella & Ray* (Jazz Live)
1949	*Ella Fitzgerald Set* (Verve)
1949	*Miss Ella Fitzgerald and Mr. Nelson Riddle* (Decca)
1950	*Gershwin Songs* (Decca)
1950	*Souvenir Album* (Decca)
1953	*Bluella: Ella Fitzgerald Sings the Blues* (Pablo)
1953	*Sweet and Hot* (Decca)
1954	*Songs in a Mellow Mood* (Decca)
1955	*Songs from "Pete Kelly's Blues"* (Decca)
1956	*Ella and Louis Together* (Laserlight)
1956	*Ella Fitzgerald Live* (Verve)
1956	*One O'Clock Jump* (Verve)
1956	*Sings Cole Porter* (Verve)
1956	*Sings More Cole Porter* (Verve)
1956	*Sings the Cole Porter Song Book, Vol. 1* (Verve)
1956	*Sings the Cole Porter Song Book, Vol. 2* (Verve)
1956	*Sings the Duke Ellington Song Book, Vol. 1* (Verve)
1956	*Sings the Duke Ellington Song Book, Vol. 2* (Verve)
1956	*Sings the Rodgers & Hart Song Book, Vols. 1–2* (Verve)
1956	*A Tribute to Cole Porter* (Verve)
1957	*Ella Fitzgerald and Billie Holiday at Newport* (Verve)
1957	*Ella and Louis Again, Vol. 1–2* (Verve)
1957	*Ella Fitzgerald at the Opera House* (Verve)
1957	*Get Happy* (Verve)

1957   *Hello, Love* (Verve)
1957   *Lady Be Good!* (Verve)
1957   *Like Someone in Love* (Verve)
1958   *Ella in Rome: The Birthday Concert* (Verve)
1958   *Ella Swings Lightly* (Verve)
1958   *Sings the Irving Berlin Song Book, Vol. 1–2* (Verve)
1958   *Sings Sweet Songs for Swingers* (Verve)
1959   *Ella Sings Gershwin* (MCA)
1959   *Ella Swings Brightly with Nelson Riddle* (Verve)
1959   *Ella Fitzgerald Sings the George & Ira Gershwin Song Book* (Verve)
1960   *Ella in Berlin* (Verve)
1960   *Ella Sings Songs from "Let No Man Write My Epitaph"* (Verve)
1960   *Ella Wishes You a Swinging Christmas* (Verve)
1960   *The Intimate Ella* (Verve)
1960   *Sings the Harold Arlen Song Book, Vol. 1–2* (Verve)
1961   *Clap Hands, Here Comes Charlie!* (Verve)
1961   *Ella in Hollywood* (Verve)
1961   *Ella Returns to Berlin* (Verve)
1961   *Ella Swings Gently with Nelson Riddle* (Verve)
1962   *Ella Sings Broadway* (Verve)
1962   *Rhythm Is My Business* (Verve)
1963   *Ella and Basie!* (Verve)
1963   *Sings the Jerome Kern Song Book* (Verve)
1963   *These Are the Blues* (Verve)
1964   *Ella at Juan Les Pins* (Verve)
1964   *Hello Dolly* (Verve)
1964   *Sings the Johnny Mercer Song Book* (Verve)
1964   *Stairway to the Stars* (Verve)
1965   *Ella at Duke's Place* (Verve)
1965   *Ella Fitzgerald* (Metro)
1965   *Ella in Hamburg* (Verve)
1966   *Ella & Duke at the Cote D'Azur* (Verve)
1966   *The Stockholm Concert, 1966* (Pablo)
1966   *Whisper Not* (Verve)
1966   *The World of Ella Fitzgerald* (Metro)
1967   *Brighten the Corner* (Capitol)
1967   *Ella Fitzgerald's Christmas* (Capitol)
1967   *Misty Blue* (Capitol)
1968   *Thirty by Ella* (Capitol)
1969   *Ella* (Reprise)
1969   *Sunshine of Your Love* (Prestige)
1969   *Ella Fitzgerald with the Tommy Flanagan Trio* (Delta)
1971   *Ella à Nice* (Pablo)

1972   *Dream Dancing* (Pablo)
1972   *Loves Cole* (Atlantic)
1973   *Carnegie Hall 1973, Vol. 1* (Jazzothèque)
1973   *Carnegie Hall 1973, Vol. 2* (Jazzothèque)
1973   *Newport Jazz Festival: Live at Carnegie Hall* (Columbia)
1973   *Take Love Easy* (Pablo)
1974   *Ella and Oscar Peterson* (Pablo)
1974   *Ella Fitzgerald Jams* (Pablo)
1974   *Ella in London* (Pablo)
1974   *Fine and Mellow* (Pablo)
1975   *Montreux '75* (Pablo)
1975   *At the Montreux Festival* (Original Jazz)
1975   *Ella Fitzgerald at the Montreux Jazz Festival 1975* (Pablo)
1976   *Ella Fitzgerald* (Pablo)
1976   *Fitzgerald and Pass Again* (Pablo)
1977   *Montreux '77* (Pablo)
1978   *Lady Time* (Pablo)
1979   *A Classy Pair* (Pablo)
1979   *Digital III at Montreux* (Pablo)
1979   *A Perfect Match* (Pablo)
1980   *Ella Abraca Jobim* (Pablo)
1982   *The Best Is Yet to Come* (Pablo)
1982   *Speak Love* (Pablo)
1983   *Let's Call the Whole Thing Off* (Pablo)
1983   *Nice Work If You Can Get It* (Pablo)
1986   *Billie Holiday & Ella Fitzgerald* (MCA)
1986   *Easy Living* (Pablo)
1988   *Wishes You a Swinging Christmas* (Polydor)
1989   *All That Jazz* (Pablo)
1989   *Starlit Hour* (Rounder)
1991   *Ella: Things Ain't What They Used to Be* (Reprise)
1991   *Ella Sings, Chick Swings* (Olympic)
1991   *Memories* (MCA)
1992   *Ella Fitzgerald* (Laserlight)
1992   *Ella with Her Savoy Eight* (ASV/Living Era)
1994   *Cole Porter Songbook, Vol. 1* (Polygram)
1994   *Lady Is a Tramp* (ITM)
1995   *Christmas with Ella Fitzgerald* (Cema Special M)
1995   *It's a Blue World* (Drive)
1995   *My Happiness* (Parrot)
1995   *My Heart Belongs to Daddy* (Musketeer)
1995   *Roseland Dance City* (Canby)
1996   *A-Tisket, A-Tasket* (Intercontinent)

1996   *Ella & Friends* (GRP)
1996   *Fabulous* (Musketeer)
1996   *First Lady of Jazz* (Leader Music)
1996   *One Side of Me* (Master Series)
1996   *Stockholm Concert* (Jazz World)
1996   *Together* (Collector's Ed)
1996   *You'll Have to Swing It* (Eclipse Music)
1997   *Rhythm & Romance* (ASV/Living Era)
1998   *Celebrated* (Magnum America)
1999   *In Budapest* (Pablo)
2000   *Ah, Wilderness* (Caedmon)
2000   *Cole Porter Songbook* (PolyGram)
2000   *Ella Fitzgerald* (Verve)
2000   *Ella: In Hollywood* (Verve)
2000   *Fitzgerald/Ellington* (PolyGram)
2000   *Forever Young, Vol. 1* (Swingtime)
2000   *Forever Young, Vol. 2* (Swingtime)
2000   *Hey, Jude* (Prestige)
2000   *In the Groove* (Buddha)
2000   *Rock It for Me* (Pilz)
2000   *That Old Black Magic* (MCA)

Resources

Are you interested in jazz history? Find out more about jazz music at the following websites:

Jazz Central Station
   <http://www.jazzcentralstation.com>
Jazz Online
   <http://www.jazzonline.com/>
JazzSite
   <http://www.teleport.com/~jazzsite/>
The Jazz Web
   <http://www.nwu.edu/jazz/internet.html>
Jazz World
   <http://www.jazzworld.com>
Red Hot and Cool Jazz
   <http://www.members.aol.com/Jlackritz/jazz/index.html>
Yahoo! Music: Jazz and Blues
   <http://www.dir.yahoo.com/entertainment/music/genres/jazz/>

Index

107

Other Titles in the Lerner Biographies Series

Agatha Christie

Alice Walker

Allan Pinkerton

Babe Didrikson Zaharias

Billie Jean King

Charles Darwin

Charlie Chaplin

Deng Xiaoping

Douglas MacArthur

Dwight D. Eisenhower

E. B. White

Emily Dickinson

Frances Hodgson Burnett

Frank Lloyd Wright

George Balanchine

Gloria Steinem

J. M. Barrie

J. R. R. Tolkien

John Muir

Julia Morgan

L. Frank Baum

Laura Ingalls Wilder

Margaret Bourke-White

Maria Montessori

Marie Curie and Her Daughter Irène

Martin Luther King, Jr.

Mother Jones

Nellie Bly

Nikola Tesla

Rachel Carson

Robert Louis Stevenson

Sir Edmund Hillary

Sylvia Earle

Photo Acknowledgments

Corbis/Bettman-UPI, pp. 2, 10, 24, 50, 74, 75, 81, 84; Glenn A. Baker Archives/Redferns/Retna Ltd., p. 6; Brown Brothers, pp. 9, 12, 19, 26, 38, 58, 62, 76, 77; Superstock, pp. 16, 46, 73; © Frank Driggs/Corbis, pp. 17, 22, 36, 44, 49; Bettman/Corbis, pp. 18, 33, 52, 55, 67, 70, 86; Shomburg Center for Research in Black Culture, p. 29; Globe Photos, Inc., p. 48; © William Gottlieb/Retna Ltd, p. 60; NBC/Globe Photos Inc., p. 64; From the Mugar Memorial Library Collection, Department of Special Collections, Boston University, p. 79; Nancy Barr/Retna Ltd., p. 87; F. Garcia/Stills/Retna Ltd., p. 89; Arnal/Stills/Retna Ltd., p. 91; Lee Engfer, p. 112.

Cover photo courtesy of Superstock.

About the Author

Katherine Krohn has written many books for young readers, including *Elvis Presley: The King, Marilyn Monroe: Norma Jeane's Dream, Princess Diana,* and *Women of the Wild West.* Ms. Krohn was born in Germany, grew up in the Detroit area, and calls the Pacific Northwest home.